Revise your Sounds

CAN YOU
Remember these sounds from Activity Books 1 and 2?

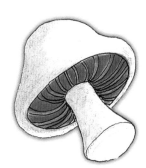

s i n d
h a
t e p
k c r m

CAN YOU
Write the letters and match the sounds to the pictures?

3

Gg

Inky wakes up and jumps out of bed. She washes quickly, then pulls the plug out and waits as the water gurgles, g, g, g, down the plughole. She is in a hurry because Snake and Bee will be arriving soon. They are all going to go out for the day.

Colour the picture!

NOW YOU CAN
Do the action and say the sound!

Action
Spiral your hand down as if water is going down the drain and say *g, g, g*.

Which of these things have the sound 'g' in them?
Join them to the letter 'g'.

Word Garden

Colour the flower's petals if there is a 'g' sound in the word.

grin

egg

dig

red

grip

grin

cat

sit

6

Put your stickers on the 'g'.

7

Oo

Inky bounces into the living room and goes over to Phonic, the computer, "o, o, o, on!" she sings as she pushes the switch. 'Good morning,' says Phonic, appearing on the screen.

Colour the picture!

NOW YOU CAN Do the action and say the sound!

Action

Pretend to turn a light switch on and off and say *O, O; O, O.*

Which of these things have the sound 'o' in them?
Join them to the letter 'o'.

NOW YOU CAN

Write the letter.
Start on the big dot!
Try different
colours!

Inky says,
"Writing
an 'o'
starts like
a 'c'!"

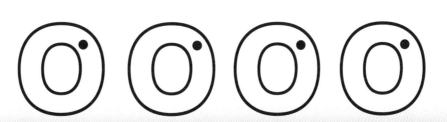

Finger Puppets

Cut out and make the finger puppets by putting glue around the outer edges but not along the bottom.

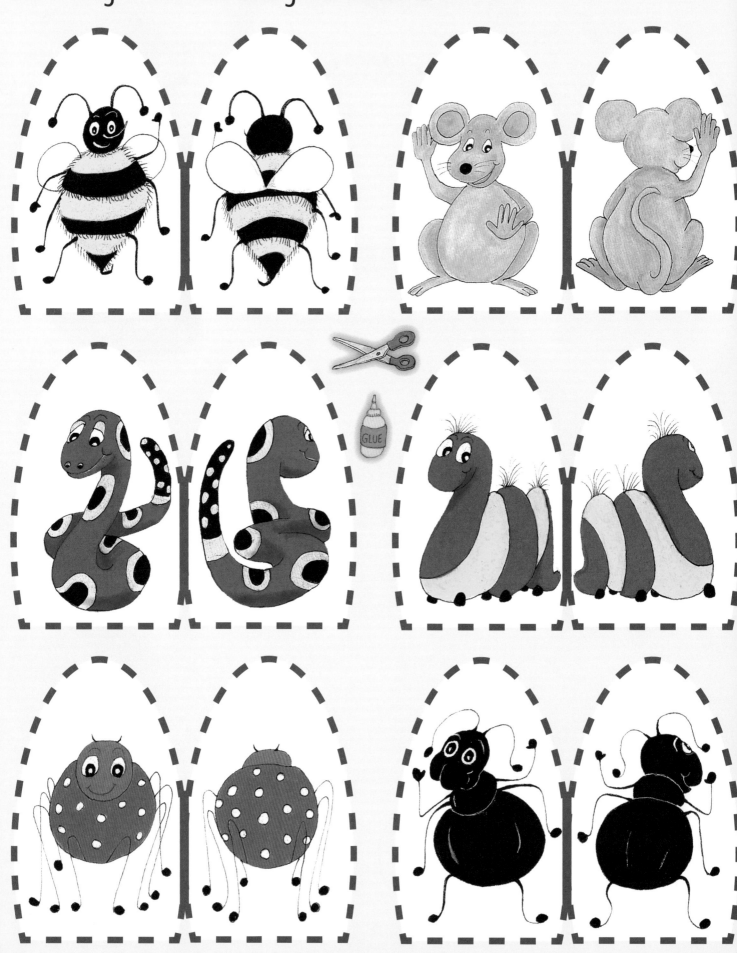

Opposites

Find the sticker that is the opposite of the picture and stick it on the facing page of the book.

on

happy

up

long

day

white

big

hot

11

U u

Inky, Snake and Bee find a good spot on the beach and unpack their things. Bee puts up a big beach umbrella, "u, u, up umbrella," she says.

Colour the picture!

NOW YOU CAN

Do the action and say the sound!

Action
Pretend to be putting up an umbrella and say *U, U, U, U*.

Which of these things have the sound 'u' in them?
Join them to the letter 'u'.

Inky says,
"Remember
the joining
tail at the
end!"

Place your stickers on the umbrellas.

It is raining and the bees have to put up their umbrellas. Read the word on the puddle and find the sticker to match.

mug

hut

sun

hug

up

duck

truck

drum

skunk

14

The 5 Vowels

There is a vowel sound in every word.
Can you use the picture clues to complete the crosswords?

Practise saying the short vowel sounds.

NOW YOU CAN Point to each finger and say the vowels.

💡 **Tips for Parents**

Short vowels affect spelling: for example, a short word with a short vowel, such as 'sack, neck, pick, lock and duck' ends in 'ck'. If there is not a short vowel sound, the word ends in 'k', such as 'look, leek, oak'.

Ll

Later Inky, Snake and Bee have a picnic. They have sandwiches to eat and lemonade to drink. Then they each have a lollipop. Snake has a lovely lime green one. "Lick the l, l, lollipop," he mutters whilst licking his lips.

Colour the picture!

NOW YOU CAN

Do the action and say the sound!

Action
Pretend to lick a lollipop and say *llll*.

Which of these things have the sound 'l' in them?
Join them to the letter 'l'.

Write the letter.
Start at the top!
Try different
colours!

Inky says,
"Hold your
pencil
correctly!"

17

Letter Dominoes

Cut out the dominoes carefully!

Save this game until you have completed the book!

s a t i p

n c m e h

r d g o u

Pages 7 & 26

n	n	n	n	t	t
p	p	p	d	s	s
d	h	m	g	g	

Page 15

Page 27

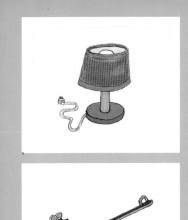

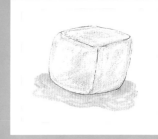

Instructions

Play this sound domino game!

1 Cut out the dominoes.

2 Deal them out.

3 The person with the Inky domino goes first.

4 Take turns matching the sounds and pictures.

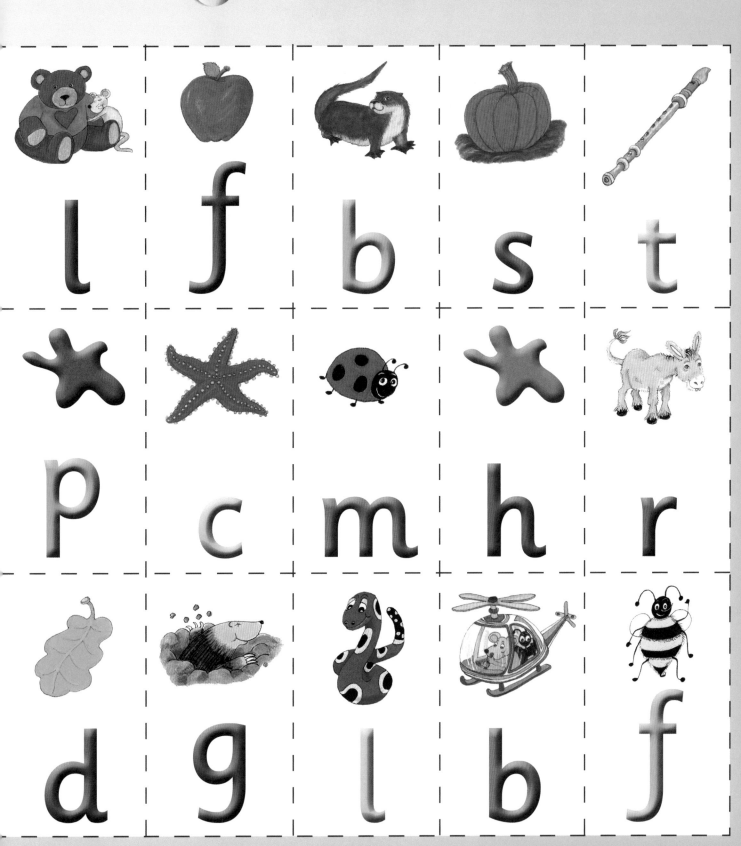

Ff

Inky, Snake and Bee build a big sandcastle with flags on the towers. Then Inky hears a funny noise, fffffff. Poor Snake - a crab has nipped his inflatable fish and it is slowly deflating.

Colour the picture!

NOW YOU CAN
Do the action and say the sound!

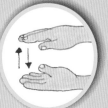

Action
Let your hands gently come together as if an inflatable fish is deflating and say *fffffff*.

Which of these things have the sound 'f' in them?
Join them to the letter 'f'.

NOW YOU CAN
Write the letter. Start at the top! Try different colours!

Inky says, "The letter 'f' is tall and has a tail!"

FRUIT BOWL

Do you know the names of these fruits?
Listen to the sound they begin with and write it underneath.

22

Letter Biscuits

90g soft unsalted butter
100g castor sugar
1 large egg
teaspoon of vanilla extract
200g plain flour
teaspoon baking powder
teaspoon salt

1. Preheat the oven to 180c or gas mark 4.
2. Cream the butter and sugar until it is soft and a pale cream colour.
3. Beat in the egg and add the vanilla extract.
4. Sieve in the flour and baking powder, add the salt and mix it together.
5. Use your hands to form the dough into a ball. If it is a bit sticky, add a little more flour.
6. Wrap the dough ball in clingfilm and place in the fridge for an hour.
7. Roll the dough out, roughly 5mm thick.
8. Cut out the letter shapes and place onto a lined baking sheet.
9. Bake for 8 to 12 mins.
10. Cool the biscuits on a wire rack and when they are cold, decorate them with icing and sprinkles.

Bb

Snake, Inky and Bee have a game of bat and ball to try and cheer Snake up. Bee hits the ball, "b, b, b," she shouts. After that they have tea before heading back home.

Colour the picture!

NOW YOU CAN

Do the action and say the sound!

Action
Pretend to hit a ball with a bat and say *b, b, b, b.*

Which of these things have the sound 'b' in them?
Join them to the letter 'b'.

NOW YOU CAN
Write the letter.
Start at the top!
Try different
colours!

Inky says,
"Hold your
pencil
correctly!"

25

Sticker Activity

Find stickers that show things with the sound 'b' in them.

Have another go at writing the letter 'b'. Remember: bat first, then bounce up and around for the ball.

Put your stickers on the 'b'.

b

b b b b

26

What's the Word?

Look at the picture and say the word, listening to each sound.
Place a letter sound sticker on each dot to spell out the word.

Anagram

Cut out the pictures and letters.

A a n
a r m g

NOW YOU CAN
Unscramble the letters to make the words.

b e d

s u n

m a p

d o g

Letter Search

It is easy to mix up 'd' and 'b'!

b 'b' starts with the bat and then bounces over for the ball.

d 'd' starts with a caterpillar 'c' then goes up for the doggy's tail.

NOW YOU CAN Colour all the b's blue. Colour all the d's red.

d	b	p	a	b	g
i	m	t	b	m	d
p	r	d	s	i	b
b	d	c	b	l	t
f	b	g	h	d	b
d	s	b	b	k	a

g o u l f b

Word and Picture Matching

NOW YOU CAN
Join the words to the pictures and later you can cut out and match.

pen

cap

hip

cat

mug

sun

log

hen

Tips for Parents
These are words using the sounds learnt so far.

lips	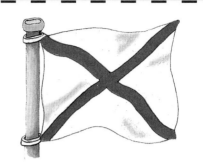
drum	
flag	
duck	
bell	
hill	

Practise Writing the Letters

Start on the dot and try to stay inside the lines!

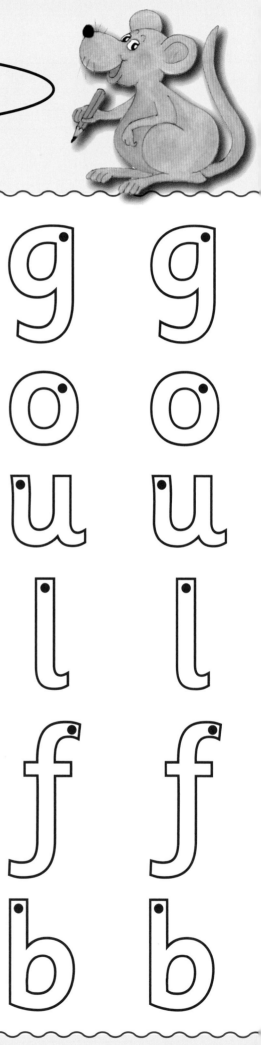

g g g g g

o o o o o

u u u u u

l l l l l

f f f f f

b b b b b

32

Sound Cards

f

b

u

l

g

o

How to use these cards

as flashcards

find the sound

copy & play pairs or snap games

make & blend words

 Tips for Parents
Cut out each card and use them in the ways suggested. Keep them and
add them to the sound cards in the other activity books.

I Know These Sounds

NOW YOU CAN
Match the sounds to the pictures.

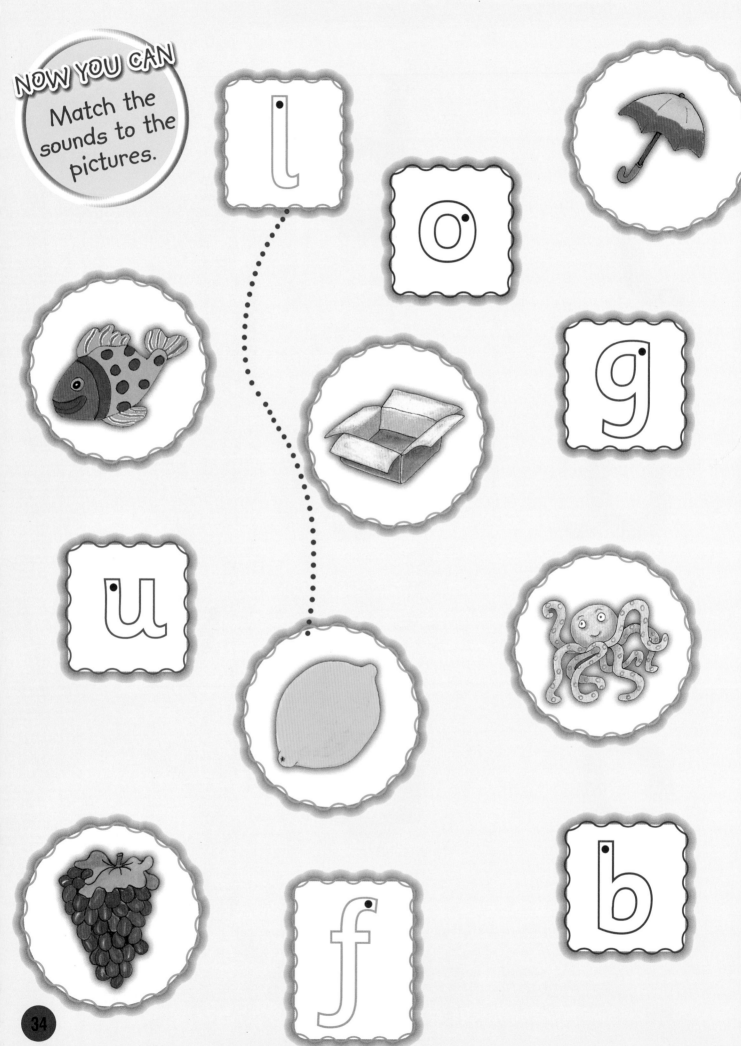

34